David Deutsch (he prefers "just Dave") has only been writing poetry for a short time, but has no intention of ever quitting. A Pennsylvania resident all his life, he has degrees from both, the University of Pittsburgh at Greensburg, and Pittsburgh Theological Seminary. Dave says poetry has value, because "it is a way to talk about those things that are most important yet hardest to explain, like love."

For Cecilia, whose wonderful soul even the greatest poems
could never fully describe.

David Deutsch

POETSY

Poetry Inspired by Cecilia

AUSTIN MACAULEY PUBLISHERS™

LONDON • CAMBRIDGE • NEW YORK • SHARJAH

Copyright © David Deutsch 2022

All rights reserved. No part of this publication may be reproduced, distributed, or transmitted in any form or by any means, including photocopying, recording, or other electronic or mechanical methods, without the prior written permission of the publisher, except in the case of brief quotations embodied in critical reviews and certain other non-commercial uses permitted by copyright law. For permission requests, write to the publisher.

Any person who commits any unauthorized act in relation to this publication may be liable to criminal prosecution and civil claims for damages.

Ordering Information
Quantity sales: Special discounts are available on quantity purchases by corporations, associations, and others. For details, contact the publisher at the address below.

Publisher's Cataloging-in-Publication data
Deutsch, David
Poetsy

ISBN 9781638295471 (Paperback)
ISBN 9781638295495 (ePub e-book)
ISBN 9781638295488(Audio book)

Library of Congress Control Number: 2022917381

www.austinmacauley.com/us

First Published 2022
Austin Macauley Publishers LLC
40 Wall Street,33rd Floor, Suite 3302
New York, NY 10005
USA

mail-usa@austinmacauley.com
+1 (646) 5125767

My thanks to the members of the Norwin Public Library,
for their encouragement and support.

Chapter 1

Because of her, not me, these sonnets are
The greatest poems one's ever written.
The others, though wondrous, fall short by far
Due to the one with whom I was smitten.
The lines of classics may be well refined
And filled with wisdom and strong emotion,
But my loved one's rarer than new gold mined
Or glinting metals from deepest ocean.
They're best because of their inspiration:
A person whose loveliness never shakes.
Therefore, they have limitless duration
In time and a firmness that never breaks.
    So may my words reflect her as a glass
    So, the mem'ry of her will never pass.

Chapter 2

There have been no poems for months on end,
And so I thought my rhymes had felt their doom,
But you have proven deeper than a friend,
And so you stand to make now new rhymes bloom.
Yes, your presence now is quite disrupting
Of a life that's casual and costs much,
And while women's charms can be corrupting,
Your dazzles, I can perceive, are not such.
You are proof that time leaves little unchanged,
Even those who boast of rigidity.
Because of you, I can now say I've ranged
From hades to heaven's felicity.
> Poems keep me from emotions' poor house,
> With you, the key to my poems' storehouse.

Chapter 3

For you, "I'm kind," is to say, "I'm natural,"
Though kindness seems what the world despises.
Some feign mercy, but for you, it's actual,
As factual as the words, "Warm air rises."
But fear, erring, is factual in my mind—
Learned thoughts, behaviors born of sorrow stay.
Nagging nerve cells warn me, "She can't be kind,"
Despite my effort to drive doubt away.
Yet in your sweet kindness, there lies patience,
Enough, for sure, to refute my mind's lies.
Your tender caring makes caution a dunce
And reminds me how faith is truly wise.
    Doubt and trusting now make a sudden switch:
    Doubt waxes poor, while trusting becomes rich.

Chapter 4

If I could rhyme in sleep, a thousand poems would be yours.
Tonight my head feels large. My mind, tiny.
Thus I fear you'll find its best fruits mere bores
And yearn for poems tuned much more finely.
I delay sleep, for this seems worth the time,
Though I know I fear the day you hear it.
So I move on, perfecting this my rhyme,
Praying you'll do more than grin and bear it.
White emptiness keeps me on the letters:
I can't leave your distant presence wanting.
My eyes see my hands as bound by fetters,
But a stronger need keeps me word hunting.
    If in reading this, pleasure you pretend,
    I hope with words not written we can mend.

Chapter 5

If you chuckle at my bumbling, does that mean you like me?
I heard kind men lose. Maybe clowns get second?
If boys' rumors have some truth, that might be,
But my mind warns this is falsely reckoned.
If I cannot be your knight, perhaps the queen would like a jester?
Can my rhymes replace the armor, my silliness, the swords?
This queen merits much—no girl can best her.
Her mouth could take my head with just two words.
No, the truth shines in your smiling sweetness:
This monarch has sincere grace and mercy!
Memories of your eyes turn me from bleakness.
Her highness bestows passage in her sea.
    I work and think and dream your clown to be,
    For then your laugh creates a laugh in me.

Chapter 6

Go and write a poem now, you small man.
Does your inwardness feel cut and irked fierce?
Massage them with some rhymes—rhyme all you can.
Your lungs might feel lighter, your stones less pierced.
Can you not endure small sorrows? Large ones?
How you lived this way, I can't understand.
Future couples will seek daughters not sons,
If our time's men consist of this your brand.
It's for your good: harshness leads to heaven.
Weak words win nothing, so hear ones harder.
Hope lies not in mercy—eat this leaven!
Gain strength through sorrow and live a martyr.
　　This wretch's guilty eyes, I cannot see,
　　For this person whom I convict is me.

Chapter 7

I wish your love toward me were not mercy,
Like a red glittered box beneath a pine.
Of men, I'm among the very worst seen,
Like a shattered bottle of common wine.
I'd rather your love be earned by some worth,
Valor, ingenious thoughts, accomplished feats.
I fear your kindness stems from grace called forth,
With pity toward my scores another beats.
But then a touch or word from you appears,
Smashing doubt with walls of thunderous power.
Then I see without fog, hear with sharp ears.
How that gaze of yours makes devils cower!
    If you lack truth, I haven't found it yet.
    Your worst untruth means naught: my heart is set.

Chapter 8

Anger burns not but is a crying thirst.
It is a desp'rate need—like want of sleep—
To drink my soul back from what stole it first,
And to remove my flaws that make you weep.
It does indeed boil—by gradation.
It first does not appear to eye or ear.
Its heat rises and defies placation.
It froths and then is balked by beauty's tear.
Hence, there is a cure for the thirst of rage:
Find another want, a sweet distraction.
Let her eyes and voice trap it in a cage,
And cause your heart to make a retraction.
    Anger is the absence of that I yen,
      A symptom of a hurt that needs to mend.

Chapter 9

There is no one thing for which you love her,
No trait she must maintain to keep your gaze.
Eyes, hair, voice, and skill make but a cover
To encapsulate a soul worth much praise.
Let her change her life. See if you grow cold.
See if great alterations change your mind.
The miner will see mud and dirt on gold,
But mud cannot reduce the miner's find.
If this one is your find do not move on.
You will not uncover one more graceful.
You will return dismayed to find she's gone.
Learn from me, a fool who's lived most wasteful.
    Let this elder's folly be for something:
    Search no more, but make this pearl your one thing.

Chapter 10

I am diff'rent—am I a hypocrite?
With you I'm soft. I speak with kind humor.
Not so with that Mister Iscariot.
So then, is my kindness just a rumor?
Don't reassure—I need to feel this guilt.
Maybe I am the evil Canaanite.
When with my foes, my brightness shouldn't wilt.
Let me atone and pray with all my might.
In so doing, I've learned how I have erred:
Against myself I've done iniquity!
I've spurned freedom and that which I preferred.
Each is their own responsibility.
> The best of what I am is yours for free,
> Because you bring about the best in me.

Chapter 11

If earth held one prom night, you'd be the queen.
Poets unite to make your description.
Writers share thoughts, and you're in ev'ry scene.
Doctors of sorrow give your prescription.
Musicians write their best: it has your name.
Sculptors labor for art that's in your form.
Athletes compete to honor you at games.
When leaders listen, your grace is the norm.
And where shall I stand amidst this glory?
I'm more than happy to fill the background.
It's enough to have you in my story.
My treasure is the one already found.
 Ev'ry other "queen" is one who poses.
 Accept these rhymes as your crown and roses.

Chapter 12

Why call it 'past' when it never passes?
When it leaves more than just marks or footprints?
It does not leave but only amasses,
Like corrupt powers who extend their stints.
For evil enjoys presence beyond flesh,
And disaster obeys no law of time.
That which was, is, will be begin to mesh,
Rendering untrue each twelve o'clock chime.
But time proves weak against other powers:
Those of love and valiance too endure.
Greatness lasts beyond unnumbered hours,
Its impact reckoned not less but far more.
    My past with you, though short, is worth repeats,
    A past my heart relives so long it beats.

Chapter 13

I wish that my senses numbered past five,
To receive more than just your touch and sight,
To meet beyond flesh, our souls to revive,
A feeling to make earth's top joys seem slight.
For sure, if I could sense past hand and ear,
And take in more of you than can be grasped,
I would run down that path without a veer,
And brace my soul for glory not surpassed.
But would you want to see my soul like that?
Mine is not so beauteous and tender.
With me you might appear as swan with bat,
And sacrifice a cent of your splendor.
 But it's enough to keep you as you seem.
 Your smallest speck makes heaven's faces beam.

Chapter 14

Don't fall in love: falling lacks intention.
It lacks direction, and its end is pain.
You, my aim, have caused no hurt to mention.
I will not fall. I'll climb to you, my gain.
Fail I to be emotive, romantic?
My reason isn't always from the heart.
Costs and other worries make me frantic.
Love wins only when lovers' minds are smart.
Life's more than order. Schedules dull the soul.
Maybe antics can be at times all right.
Forty diamond years beat ninety of coal,
Even if they contain a dose of plight.
    I therefore offer love from heart and brain,
    One the most gifted actors fail to feign.

Chapter 15

What shame, my hands do naught but put down words.
At times they use a tool for snow or leaves,
But ha! Let's see them fish or hunt for birds.
And look! These arms are good for books, not heaves.
She must want one who knows the arts of men.
All my thinking, writing, to her is lame.
It's true for sure, so I'll not write again.
Let my paper perish; I'll find new aim.
At last, I know not to replace, but add.
Both sorts of work have meaning of their own.
Work of arm and spirit are to be had
By everyone whose frames and minds have grown.
If I do naught but her felicity,
　　Then I've done my responsibility.

Chapter 16

Love is fright'ning, as all power can be.
Even scripture has it that evil loves:
Love of money, it confesses, damns thee.
Power begets peril, like playful shoves.
The devil, yes, can marry. And bandits.
Pure hearts in love often become victims.
The wisest minds, when stressed, can lose their wits.
And love's a consumer, who'll buy your limbs.
Listen to this poet's clowning ranting!
What silliness I declare with style!
Your loving frown soon has me recanting,
As though love put my wisdom on trial.
    No matter how long I might delay it,
    I promise you now one day I'll say it.

Chapter 17

For all my skill in words, I can't state love.
Like the name of God, it can't be spoken.
It's gentle strength, like Holy Spirit's dove.
But strength, like Christ's body, can be broken.
Love is diverse, full of contradiction.
Fear, joy, anger, and wonder are its parts.
It's a pleasant sail with rocky friction.
Love's body is caressed with painless darts.
I wish the feeling that you cause inside,
But I loathe nervousness, yet that's the one.
I race toward you, while trying to hide.
I embrace the passion I want to shun.
 Despite its swarm of poetic diction,
 I know—as fact—love is not a fiction.

Chapter 18

Wiser in the ways of women and men
Am I now than the I you never met.
Would you even have talked to the me then?
What I would have said is anyone's bet.
How red face making my dumb slowness felt.
How false sounding my true life stories are.
Trying to bait a hook or fix a belt—
(Oh crim!)—my lame attempts so far from par.
I'd trust in fairies before my old thoughts.
Thankfully, I have you instead to trust.
Though my brain's bulb—I think—is short some watts,
I know this as truth that you are my must.

    My thanks to you for your dearness so sweet.
    My prayer: you like the me we've yet to meet.

Chapter 19

Seven hundred love songs are not enough.
Ten thousand such poems fail you justice.
And I know these poems make me less tough,
But I'll risk it, if it's your cost to kiss.
Yes, it's true these love rhymes have grown staler,
So I'll just have to write better for you.
Songs now sound as though made by a wailer,
So I'll sing new ones for fear I bore you.
Words and numbers do not express all things,
Least of all your delighting, wholesome grace.
While the classic lyrics may have pleased kings,
Your merit is a much more special case.

Now let me work for finer lines than these,
Your ears and tender-minded heart to please.

Chapter 20

Why can I not have anger without rage?
I do not oppose anger—it's healthy,
But why has it no regulator, gauge?
Why must all be either poor or wealthy?
Anger need not always be ill feeling.
Wrath only is the sickness, the extreme.
Like burnt skin, wrath turns my spirit peeling.
The pests, not as large as they seem.
But—good news!—there is a middle balance.
Come forth, present yourself, the golden mean.
Your eyes kill my rage faster than a lance.
But an injustice makes just anger seen.

    As teeth are good for both snarl and smile,
    Angry feelings help both the just and vile.

Chapter 21

Love has many meanings, and here is one:
"I want to go with you through suff'ring times."
A friend is but a toy if just for fun—
Worse if they're useless to you past their primes.
I leave, when it loses utility,
A tool, some object, but never a friend.
Should I, then my soul is futility,
A garden of bleeding weeds none can tend.
If paradise excludes you, I'll decline.
When Adam farmed thorns, at least he had Eve.
I'll drink water with you. Forget the vine.
If the mansion lacks you, I'll take my leave.
    I say the truth, by honor of my blood:
    You, most dear, can make Eden out of mud.

Chapter 22

Respect is wishing one's view of me good,
While love includes it but is much, much more.
Respect's a show, not acting as I would,
But love makes the good show my real life core.
I deserve, it's true, a lazy lowlife,
So I'm reduced to that when not in love,
But you deserve one who gives you no strife.
So then, I've changed myself to that thereof.
Change is challenged by the stress of living.
The world, it seems, wishes my conduct bad.
I prefer you need not be forgiving,
But enjoy such joys like no one's yet had.
　　This year I start with the words, "I love you,"
　　For in this life there've been none above you.

Chapter 23

Lovers are frank, flattery comes from fools.
Avoid the one who tells you you're spotless.
Lovers feel free, for they follow good rules.
The arrogant think much but are thoughtless.
No need to advertise, dazzle, amaze.
You have no forces of competition.
I don't do returns; my price will not raise.
I find you a most fruitful commission.
You have some trait, I do not know its name;
But it makes you a peerless companion.
It consecrates you, though all are the same.
If all are pits, you are the grand canyon.
> Only you make an average day thrilling.
> Only you make a lifetime fulfilling.

Chapter 24

It's pride to want my name in history?
Then why do you urge me to strive so hard?
Don't I play Mozart to match his glory?
Practice my rhyming to exceed the bard?
No, it's *your* pride that pushes me yet pulls.
You wish your offspring great but not greater.
I'd rather be plain than one of your tools,
A commoner than your ego's waiter.
Still I have no joy in your displeasure,
Nor do I wish to see someone suffer.
In liberty, family's still a treasure,
But the practical is often rougher.

    The ideal comes but only in small parts,
    Even to the masters of family arts.

Chapter 25

If there's a part of you that's unseeing,
It's your strength to be a good forgiver.
You may change the most cynical being,
Making him exalt in life, not shiver.
I once said I'd erase my history,
Start again, all acts and traits forgotten.
I see, through you, growth's not a mystery.
I can endure human life's most rotten.
I have no need to be recreated,
But to grow in love and strength-—that's the goal.
As our time goes, I grow more elated
To see the life I once thought sorrow stole.
    Truly, you are the one least blind in heart,
    For you alone saw how to make this start.

Chapter 26

What has occurred is beaut'eous and bizarre.
It's strange to know that these things can happen.
When loved, you feel more handsome than you are.
You humbly feel the best, a ten of ten.
There's a fearfulness to love like ours:
The sense it's not the real world but a trance
Or that unseen cracks will fell these towers.
Oh, that time will never disrupt this dance!
If there's something in this world that's mystic,
It's this, that two can rightly equal one.
Did we decide, or did fate's power pick?
When we die, will the bond we share be done?

    The more we spin as one around life's wheel,
    The more I think, perhaps, that magic's real.

Chapter 27

How strange, till now I knew not what you are:
I've decided you are made of music,
For music restores my mind with each bar,
And keeps my soul from becoming too sick.
It's not only your voice but *all* that's you:
Ev'ry cell is a melody to hear!
With ev'ry blink, you make my life brand new.
Your silent songs make my darkest depth cheer.
Yes, you must be music. I have no doubt.
How else could you make beauty a feeling?
Your words and deeds, the notes of wisdom shout.
Your hands hold lyrics of mental healing.
    It's true, your major and your minor keys
    Affect my feeling state with perfect ease.

Chapter 28

Old faces stay in me for decades still.
But I'd trade them for just your countenance.
I recall long lists that few others will.
But your stories deserve mem'ry's last dance.
Yes, if time must clean out mem'ry's casket—
Making me aged in mind as well as skin—
I pray your legacy avoids its net,
Even if all others must leave the bin.
My mem'ry's like an attic full of trash.
Why not clean and let you take residence?
Let the prickly past be reduced to ash.
You may claim the storehouse of my mind hence.
    I joy in that our lives have just begun.
    In you, my all is made to be but one.

Chapter 29

Though now apart from you I've been confined,
I've no reason for anger or despair.
I can accept with ease to be resigned,
Despite this situation far from fair.
For I've learned the art of trusting, waiting.
We are still bound even without contact.
The thought to touch again, how elating!
Your image is, till then, as firm as fact.
Time and distance do not move my feeling
For a platonic friend, so much less you.
Love, shapeless, can reach through heaven's ceiling.
We have what space and time cannot undo.
    The you of sight and sound I do prefer,
    But to the you of mem'ry I defer.

Chapter 30

Why is night seen as the time of romance?
It is a time, to me, of dark and cold.
No, day, says I, is the best time to dance.
That is the time when life looks bright as gold.
Daytime is more like you, full of warm light.
Eve'ning doesn't feel like you in the least.
At night I can't see you, try as I might.
The dawn brings with it your sight from the east.
Don't settle for the moon: yours is the sun,
For you need a symbol more radiant.
You are the light that makes my night undone,
My heart's summer for which I'm ebullient.
 Like a comfort fire in winter's snow,
 You provide the warmth in a sea of woe.

Chapter 31

I think mother nature's a magician.
How else could she craft a marvel like you?
And father time, no mathematician;
For your youthful beauty shall last past due.
I think thus for you defy my knowledge:
My time with you, more wondrous than I thought.
I am held to you as though by a wedge,
Like a prey desiring to be caught.
I can't view you as just atoms jumbled.
Your source and essence must be much finer.
Through you, my stubbornness has been humbled.
Could unguided chance produce this shiner?
    Like an ideal pulled from works of fiction,
    These months together surpassed prediction.

Chapter 32

This is what I face with you, most adored:
You are easy to please, hard to impress.
You boast high standards but are not fast bored,
Like a kind and humble queen or empress.
For the one, I am most thankful, relieved:
You've spared me kindly a life frustrated.
For the other, I wrongly feel aggrieved:
I should not need assurance restated.
I love that love is for us no contest:
No need to outperform the other one.
It'd hurt us both to try to prove who's best,
For then should I beat all, I would have none.
    Nothing feels quite so marvelous as this,
      That when we are ourselves there's naught amiss.

Chapter 33

I'd rather be the answer to your prayers
Than have my own supplications realized.
What irony, the world's providence dares
To prize you with one who's not himself prized.
What honor, truly, to have this mission:
To work for your long life and great gladness.
I will be the well you throw your wish in,
And I still would even if I had less.
These words would be ironic and bitter
If spoken to someone other than you;
But it's no jest. All your doings glitter
With the very brightest of every hue.
    So varied and eminent are your charms
    That I'll consent to live inside your arms.

Chapter 34

When happy, I must write of you, dear one.
Like all feelings, joy must not be stifled.
The thought of you: the one to which I run
With a love that is not to be trifled.
When sad, I'll write about some other thing,
As you deserve the gladdest I can grant.
The feeling you give rises me to sing,
While other feelings bring me low to chant.
Yes you, dear one, inspire no sad love songs.
Even should you, it would make no diff'rence,
For your heart is the one for which mine longs,
And that longing does not die with offense.
    So when I next feel glad, and bright, and well,
    It's then I'll have for you more rhymes to tell.

Chapter 35

I search for new things to liken to you
But find so little to describe your grace.
Nature's marvels belong beneath your shoe,
And human art falls short beside your face.
The truth is that you stand as one unique.
Hence, comparison is without a point.
You reign apart from all else one might seek.
I feel this truth for sure with ev'ry joint.
I am forced, then, just to say that you are,
With that being the compliment supreme.
From your name, other compliments fall far,
As though you were the ideal of a dream.
    So now you are the standard for all those
    Who would be the one who most brightly glows.

Chapter 36

Cut off from you, I exist but don't live,
As life is more than food, and drink, and sleep.
Daily rhythms cannot match what you give,
And debaucheries make existence cheap.
I'm as grateful for you as for shelter,
Heat, light, air, clothing, all necessity.
Though the sun's bright warmth might make me swelter,
Yours won't exceed essentiality.
I yearn to scale the distance between us
And make our bond an ever tighter knot.
The path to you can't be too onerous,
And should it prove, still our love shall ne'er rot.
    You need not run to meet me in the middle:
    For me, the run to you is always little.

Chapter 37

I know someone who's not as sweet as you,
And that's ev'ryone else I've ever met!
When they turn rotted red, you stay bless'd blue,
Always the one who causes no regret.
Though not all prove frightful, coarse, or fickle,
They still fall short of the standard you've raised.
Your goodness flows in floods, others' trickle.
Some met the par, but only you amazed.
I don't look for redeeming qualities
In you, since, to me, you do not need them.
All wear the hats of mediocrities,
But for you is reserved the diadem.
    However, does there exist such a crown
    That would rightly suit one of such renown?

Chapter 38

On the day when all sights and sounds dissolve
To dark and quiet, I wonder, with fear,
'What changes will that moment then involve?
Will I lose all powers of eye and ear?'
The chief fear: will I ever again feel?
Let my body rot with all my senses,
But may my love and reason, please, stay real.
Let them stay no matter what commences.
Oh, let my memory of her not fade
Like all other things I have seen and heard.
Whether I go beyond or am remade,
For love's sake, death mustn't speak the last word.
    To breathe beyond this place of flesh and time
    Is worth it for just your mem'ry sublime.

Chapter 39

The woman I love is not my weakness
But the one from whom I gain bravery;
For there's greatness in embracing meekness
And cause to turn aside from knavery.
No, I do not have a weakness for her:
With her I feel a strength like mountains' stone;
And in the worst of places that we were
Is where that strength in finest brilliance shone.
Therefore, love is strength, more than sixty suns,
More than the power of celestial orbs;
And ours, more durable than anyone's.
As time moves on, the more strength love absorbs.
    Let the evils of the world try to break
    Our bond and see it's true it will not quake.

Chapter 40

My youth's eyes gloried in adversity,
Thinking manhood's honor was the payment.
Pride's feet hurried with thoughts of victory,
Not once at all recalling what shame meant.
Hubris proved the axe of adversity.
Glory's promise I found to be a ploy.
I proved not grandiose but a pity.
It was I adversity did destroy.
But loss created something new—a space,
An open spot my foes could not foretell,
To which another one of me did race
To ring Easter morning's victory bell.
>   So now that life appears to have no seam,
>   I pray your love will help me build this dream.

Chapter 41

After a day with you, I see only
What is good about the world of humans.
My darkest doubt is declared a phony
And my pettiness reduced to ruins.
There's a piece of sunlight that's not in space,
Because God put it on earth in your form.
It overshines all things horrid and base,
Making me forget when love's not the norm.
But then I'm pulled away from you by chance
Or duty's beckon. Then pessimism
Comes again with the sharp strength of a lance,
And humans seem trapped in nihilism.
    But I can end now on this happy note:
    Your light's even greater than what I wrote.

Chapter 42

I believe that love begins with wonder,
The curiosity of impressed youth,
For love tears expectations asunder,
And with light roughness reveals all untruth.
Is it true, then, that with advancing age?
The joys of learning more of love must cease?
I forbid, for it's known by every sage
That knowledge just makes one's wonder increase.
Your charm lies in my not comprehending—
Why are your nat'ral acts so engaging?
Why should you bedazzle me with tending?
To daily matters, my heart encaging?
How did you obtain this strength of power
To make me long for your prison tower?

Chapter 43

While wicked men work to feed their pride,
To ease existence and endure no strife,
The true man's work makes better the inside,
To live a life that is no fake of life.
Temptation flows from the ever large dark,
The cosmos that makes men's smallness quiver.
Petty pleasures and selfishness cry, "Hark!"
If men believe their timeline a sliver.
Even the weakest can't be a pity,
Though very slight to me my power seems.
Causal chains link small with enormity,
As nature feeds the sea with tiny streams.
    I wish my years to be the good for each.
    Extend your hand, and I will meet your reach.

Chapter 44

Today I write for one I love to greet.
Her name has been added to a small chest
Of those with whom I've shared that special heat,
That love which makes me lose self-interest.
Even overflowing days of duty
Have time enough for many thoughts of you.
Indeed, such thoughts help block out the moody,
Which, confessedly, overcome me too.
I feel, as though, a hand of cruel control
Reaches for me, even if imagined.
Reddening stress, anger, shame take their toll.
Depression pummels me with icy wind.
But when these try to take me in a snatch,
    The stronger thought of you is there to match.

Chapter 45

Because I remembered you as I lied
In sleepless night but hours ago in bed,
It is now—this morning—my hand's untied
To pen fresh words about you from my head.
When time apart from you builds up in length,
So does time away from poems' paper.
Without your clear mem'ry, my rhymes lack strength;
My creativity starts to taper.
And I'm sorry my art is not the best;
I know you merit a finer poet.
If you had not grace, I'd not pass your test,
But I'll try hard, for to you I owe it.
    And yet, a part of you stays always fresh.
    In dreams, our souls may ever still enmesh.

Chapter 46

My mind's stream leads to rapids much hotter
And more turbulent than a lava pool.
Your stream leads away from raging water
And to the soothing lake that's calm and cool.
I want your lake yet run to the rapid
Like a child choosing sugar not meat.
Why do I baptize myself in vapid
Waters when you have those healthy and sweet?
And why drink from aging and cracked clay jars
When you possess the holiest of grails?
Why not swim with you under private stars
Instead of letting sea storms tear my sails?
    When I feel the hot agony of stress,
    I will imagine you to make it less.

Chapter 47

If you appear so flawless to these eyes,
Which can't focus but only make rough blurs,
How heaven-like and glor'ious I surmise
You must look, like gold of richest emp'rors.
If my two ears, which fail consistently,
Sense this sweetness in your encaging voice,
Then good ears must hear you with greater glee,
Which, if up to me, would be my first choice.
And if this calloused and talentless hand
Feels such stunning power when clasped by yours,
A strong one's feeling, I can't understand.
How you cause all others to seem such bores!
    All those whose senses see you as you are
    I envy, for I sense you from afar.

Chapter 48

My eyes, it seems, see more than what is there:
They see futures I hope will not exist.
However unlikely, to me they glare
As if with reddened killer's eyes and fist.
I think, then, to your healthy influence,
And that makes my pessimism retreat.
How strong you must be to inflict such dents
In my unthinking, hardened mind of meat.
Therefore, my future won't be of regret.
My future is something better than that
It would have been, and so I'm in your debt
For the mem'ries that have made my heart fat.
    I'll never know what time plans to unveil,
    So may your love keep me from falling frail.

Chapter 49

Is it enough to live only to live?
Is life the end or just the means to it?
Is this thought too cowardly to forgive,
Or is this the proper way to view it?
I fear, confessedly, where great sadness
Might drive me to. To snatch another's joys?
I deny I chose this—I want gladness!
Do I exist to be one of God's toys?
There is one redemption from this evil:
I remember the hope you made me feel.
You taught me once to avoid upheaval,
So I know a warm future could be real.
    Even though it wasn't your intention,
    Your presence gave brightness beyond mention.

Chapter 50

I miss what was, but too, what might have been.
I wonder, 'Was our union a foretaste
Of everlasting gladness or its kin?'
If so, was our time spent but a small waste?
I refuse it! How can any joyous
Wonder be marred by having bound'ries?
The moon's smallness makes it not less glorious—
Still a product of the godly foundries.
I will no more dream of alternatives
Or count the imperfections that led here.
Power is what my mem'ry of you gives,
Enough to shed only the shorter tear.
    Your words and works are not that which sank you
    But my cause for humbly saying, "Thank you."

CPSIA information can be obtained
at www.ICGtesting.com
Printed in the USA
BVHW072358110123
655994BV00011B/674